GH00836408

Nerve Centre

Banana dress, he wears as he walks in the prevailing wind of the beach.

He knows too well that a day is fleeting,

crushed in an instant like a soda can.

And he goes through town walking very quickly inland from the sea and cove.

He walks over bridges and steps on storm drains.

The bells of townspeople Morris dancers follow him everywhere

as he retreats beneath rumbling skies to degenerate old churchyards.

His dress becoming a wispy and flamboyant skirt,

a golden thread.

In the churchyard as the grave keeper.

That is his job.

What a strange town.

Hiding under graveyard trees that grow

very thick and large with free branches,

digging up muck,

tossing it filled with bones over his shoulder.

Rabbits in the graveyard.

This town with all its dead people,

the demography forever trending towards old and white

and dispassionate conservatism,

have entrusted their bones,

corpses to someone so glorious.

Everything so disparate in this graveyard,

him the completely bespeckled, all-knowing oneness of man.

Like the Buddha.

Looking at him you come to understand he is not only a grave keeper,

but a treasurer,

arbiter of the whole town and its traditions,

like a guard at the Tower of London.

He is not ideological but relentlessly scientific

in his understanding of past and present.

He wishes to influence the long-term,

sees everything as malleable, an institution, and men and women cast in nickel,

lead.

To fall in love with the man in the banana dress,

to sail out to enveloped, murky islands of disease,

eating exotic cuisine and dirty-cheap tacos,

and stand in the castle halls of mirrors.

Across the room from each other,

the spices still on our lips,

jousting in a prism of royal glass.

That is the nerve centre of all I want.

Blonde/Blond Memories

Flaming blonde youth

under spirals of mercury.

The house is a narrow house with multiple stories.

God puts his hand on the window.

Angels dwell in Albion.

Out of my mind,

on the horse in the mountains

in Argentina

in the lightning storms,

dashing through at highspeed.

A landscape painter.

The great ultra-monolithic cosmic struggle

of trying to get on with life

with his English memory in my brain.

Must push through.

Now changed from the days of cheap,

vulgar,

immediate intercourse at his,

the other,

fluorescent fortress.

Everything is so slow,

unchanging.

Even those in the highest places.

on panels at climate summits,

seem to lack urgency, obsession.

They have no driving instinct.

She restricts my spirit.

She, the laundrette,

who promulgates a code of cosy future,

no risk.

She was weak.

She must make others weak.

The engine must be sustained

for those unwilling to remove total freedom.

Bloody Mind of Primitivism

I refuse to die, at home alone with drunk sleepy father.

I will take every treatment.

I will fill my lungs with air.

My body is stretched and replenished

as I walk through the wormhole

back to mystical nineteenth century Wales,

burning farmhouse,

mother in cloths and rags dropping baby down wishing
well.

I refuse to die and I refuse to sit still.

I'm only fourteen

but I nurse a burning affection for the twenty-six-year-
old man

who drives the milk truck,

and who one day I will invite in and trap with a skeleton
key.

At the farmhouse, there is a secret door which goes to a basement,

where there are innocent victims chained to the walls.

Their eyes shoot through me.

If only I could reach through the square and grey pale of time and free them.

I refuse your questions, your answers.

I refuse your mother's expressionless responses and desire.

Your beautiful friend with his bayonet,

who I was once shackled to and who I thought would be his own medicine for me

and who I could envision travelling with

to shag on English Civil War church stones,

he will soon yearn for me.

He will yearn for me until he is mad,

buckled,

a hopping frog. And he will forego his amphetamine

and his painting tools.

And when he does, I will refuse him also,

pregnant with feverish desire.

I will not die, but I will gladly be forgotten.

I will disappear into the icy, misty vulgarity of all of time.

Existentialist Pub Drinking

Driver's licenses over dry out house counters in the middle of an empty street, dartboards on the walls and stubborn patrons, girl behind bar who does not ID, beer, beer, beer, French fries. Out in the pub and who's that coming up the garden path but his Highness King of Norway? and carrying a shopping bag with paper in it and wearing his crown. Up to the bar and girl, ordering beer, outside sitting with me. He says hello and I ignore him. Too tired for this affair. Never sleeping, always awake, needing to hold eyes open. I am troubled by dreams and thoughts of lost friendships with people I was once passionate with and warm toward. I remember our black dog from childhood. What perspective to approach things from? When is it right to be easy going and when should one be grandiose? Back inside pub and followed by His Majesty. More beer. I say how is wife keeping? He says ok. I remark that we are both old, forty, encyclopaedic. Perhaps it is time to close up tent, what gets better past forty? But then again he is royalty and perhaps he wields an altogether different perspective. One mustn't pre-judge or assume or try to make out another person when they do not even know themselves. Pauper or King, it is all just as transitory as dust and rags, bid it all goodbye. Drink at the pub, make novels on napkins and goopy beermats. Forget foolish and corrupting self-love, relegate thyself to the lowest extremity and die there thankful for never having gotten a taste of coming up any higher. Live and die entirely unknown and luxuriating in self-acceptance.

Leisure Time

Leisure time out in Paris garden cafes, with maybe four hundred co-patrons, drinking tea and all wearing hoop skirts, six friends and I. It is all so much better than working and I try not to think about how I'll be back and slaving away tomorrow. We are trained to work very hard at things that don't matter. This is what matters. April, garden. Even us in among it all, all five hundred, all however many billion on the earth, we aren't what matters. In the eyes of nature we're still strangers, even when kissing and making love. We are really not worth a dime. It is the tree and the leaves and by God the sky, holy Jesus, that are the most permanent of things. It's Paris, in which there is vested the very headwinds of all world history. That's where it is. And I, I am quite incongruent here, which is how one should always be. One is more beautiful when he or she does not fit. Romance is one thing but romance for most people is too easy and in our age of inward snideness most people do not desire true romance. What gives real value is loneliness or separation, not quite saying things right so no one can ever pin it down. Even out with friends it is the dodging of each other that is most quintessential. That's the thrill. But the world is both overt and tacit. How does anyone have the strength to steward themself through it? But Paris is nice. Much nicer than the package holidays of youth bought from degenerate British newspapers, when I was hollered at in between caravans in the mud and denigrated. Paris is where you can be you and not share it and that is the most truthful thing you can be to yourself.

England 2036

South Coast of England,

the deepest point of the oily productivity puzzle.

Needs a good dose of serum.

The sky is streaked with black clouds,

the frontiers of human ability,

human worth are languishing.

We have sex and then look out of the window.

There is nothing else to do.

A seagull lands.

The unipolar world is connected on demented globalised
wires.

All the hollowed-out people,

in those hollowed-out, formerly industrial countries.

Me and her are radicals,

we look at these waters and still see Lord Nelson,

jubilant privateers.

History scuttles down these cybernetic drainpipes.

The husband and the wife outside,

who must both work four jobs each to support

their benefit-capped kids

with unhealthy fat foods,

under the order of the flaming insect robot the state
crammed into their walls.

British state,

guarding over this ever urban-sprawled Garden of Eden,

with its High Tory ruffians.

You can hear the bailiff creepy crawlers take their fridge
away.

Daddy will have to pay next time.

The van pulls out.

The caterer government that fails on its train and boats,

that is running from its own infrastructure.

Ready to burn the garden down to ash.

There is no ability to change it,

that much is clear, distinguishable.

Even in the solitary flaccid dick pic sent prematurely on
the dating app,

there is all the evidence you need of people given up on a framework,

straddled into genitalia market fundamentalism.

Me and her conclude there are no social solutions.

That life is uneventful goo and eggshells.

We go to bed again.

Father and Daughter

New boots purchased from shop window.

Boots that add a very definite inflection to a way of walking.

The father was here today and so was the daughter,

the both of them as large as walruses,

wearing sheepskin.

Well, there is a tendency to provoke me,

at the very least that's how I read it,

me so weird and divine,

me thrashing about with instruments and sitting on lawn chair,

cramped,

skeletal on public grass.

Hair in eyes.

There is no desire from me.

The sun is blotted out,

I am impassive, dispassionate, quiet to all.

As the day goes on and I forget about the father and daughter,

I dream only of the sea and remember its musical, desperate qualities.

My boots become webbed, diving footwear.

The sea is the great lawless place of fraternity,

lavish equality and carefree attitudes,

democratic and rich discussion,

utilitarian exchanges of frothing desire.

There are wedding bells today

and I think forward to a possible wedding day also.

Groom,

groom,

me,

perhaps one day

out of the prying eyes of the father and daughter who now walk their dog.

Rosy Tomorrows

The pelvic bone is ground down.

My head is a redhead.

Lying in bed with his fat lips

like velvet sponge chairs.

Minds empty,

debanked.

My parents believe in marriage,

but I do not think about it at all.

Rather, I fill up ashtrays and fuck

and dance to old muzak.

What do they know?

Who is the predictor of perfect behaviours?

When I think of them, I think of all kinds of things.

How they will behave, what they will do,

is as much a matter of the way the wind is blowing as it
is anything else.

I sit with him,

another person so airy and aloof,

that nothing worries him.

Bedhead.

Nothing should ever be a worry.

Fuck worrying.

I draw on him,

enter into possession of his spirit

and shrink into carefree quiet.

In the afternoon,

we eat boiled ham with salt and garnish.

My mouth is spoiled and dry and I pick my nose.

I lay on the bed,

belly-down

and reading and waiting for time to pass,

for things to happen.

Life is spat in thick and vulgar

breaths of mucus and sperm and rigid sex

where spines break.

Then it must return to quiet and smelling fingernails,

engaging in only the most boring of tasks
at will.

It is on conveyor belt, churning.

I wait around for bladder to fill,

wait around for good times.

Gate

There's that beautiful boy with the beautiful eyes. Well, I'd go to him with love offerings if he only would only smile and let me know. But me I'm too silly nervous and I won't push open his gate or go to his door. And him, he's too indestructible, the words from his mouth are fermented with gold. You don't dare touch him, someone like that. A part of me wonders if he even sees me, leaning against the wall, on his phone, unaware entirely. Boys who make a mockery of cowards and who cannot be resisted, I think they are the greatest cause of my shame. What about yesterday when he came in looking so cute in his fisherman's hat? Wasn't that something? One day there will be a reckoning for people like me, and even more glory heaped on him. I analyse every decision and gesture I make like I do with him, and I am left doubting how I draw water from a dispensary with him sitting far away with legs crossed and studying and maybe but most likely not watching me and me not looking up to check because it might shatter the dreams. It's a real curse.

Suffrage

I was an alcoholic artist,

I was depressed.

The results of the plebiscite had not gone my way.

They had voted to ban artists.

It turned my stomach.

So I went down the road with the dust in the air

and sunglasses on,

and stopped in the pub.

I thought perhaps I had made too much of a play

of the results.

The majority had voted.

The majority are right.

It is true,

the artist is not a liberator.

The artist makes the tiny things the gentry play around
with.

Surely if the artist didn't exist

the revolution could go ahead

with bayonets and statues tumbling.

Bourgeois culture would collapse under its own boredom.

All art is in the graveyard, middle class homes.

I walk out the pub, drunk,

with Heaven and Hell above and below me on the London street.

I am mugged on the roundabout at knifepoint.

My wallet and phone are stolen.

I cannot even cancel my card.

I lie on the floor.

I get up and stand on a green hill.

I wait there.

Airport

They are minimised in this castle and do not know it. But
we are smaller with total sovereignty. Smaller in
wasteland airport café, looking out at pure white
desolation. Sun not coming up, thick clouds and thick
fog. The roar of jets, hard, in the runway skyline.
Transient bliss in separation from the rest of the world,
from culture, climate, robotics. You can see why big
transnational conglomerates rock up in places like this
for reasons beside transfer pricing and tax status. It is
faceless corporate alienation. Indifferent but also cynical.
They do everything in this café. Spice buns, lattes, chips,
bean burritos. I drink an Americano by the window.
Soon I'll be up in that sky tube, that long and thin air
manatee that cruises at 30,000 feet, trapped for nine
hours in transition, permanent coffee-spiked alertness
and drowsiness. I finish my coffee and go to leave. Walk
past the quiet and middle-aged tables where the clientele
all bear flat shark faces. I trip on a chair left out of place
and fall in the aisle into a crushed burrito dropped on the
floor. No one gets up to help. When I stand there are
only stares.

Ice Cream

Going outside and down the street with a fountain. To the ice cream parlour, dressed, regaled in brown tailored suit with lapel and tie. Ordering a bottomless, three scoop mountain of sundae. Sitting down at table with it and crossing legs as it melts down the thin, tubular glass in cloudy streaks onto the napkin at the base. The punishing sunshine and the much-appreciated air conditioning of here. Fountain outside linking to a complicated water installation that extolls gratitude, however briefly, for some of the town planning, money powers of local government. Me with my thin spoon, dangling at the edge, looking like a doctor with surgical, forensic instruments, eating the cherries off the top with nothing but gladness. The place has the smell of an ice cream shop, new, fresh, oddly corporate in its modernity, but still they've won me over, capitalism has me hooked on its freezer, milkshake pheromones. Picking my way through the ice cream like digging a grave in a graveyard, finding Yorick, to the bottom of the wishing well. Other people perhaps looking at me and looking away again. No one really pays any attention which is a freeing thing. Then up off the table to thank the staff, some of whom double up and work in the Mexican restaurant down the way. What a way to start a morning.

Radio Station, North England 1939

Northern radio station,

every day seems like a miracle.

The war machines are pointed at each other

across the valley.

The radio station studio with molten black carpets

and lined walls,

enough to melt you in the purple summer heat,

flushed,

extending through to the first week of 1930s September.

I am a sweaty mess

at the microphone.

A woman walks into the studio,

elegant, streaking summer,

legs like stilts of black rock.

Beautiful red, flashes of colour.

I think of fluffing my hair,

but it doesn't matter.

I am a mess,

look like a mess.

But to hell with it,

we are entering abyss,

sliding into fog.

I look a mess and do not waste away worrying.

Courtyard

Running away from photos at school and heading to stony courtyard. All alone and looking around, a solitary tree, planted in a brick pot. So peaceful. I sit on the bench and cross my legs, cross them tight and place hands, folded, over lap. Beautiful blue socks and beautiful amber shoes I took off walking this morning, leaning on a lamppost, to pour the stones from my shoes. How glorious I must have looked to driver, pulling out of driveway. I sit on bench and wait for time to pass, getting warmer now, you can enjoy being outside, need an umbrella. The courtyard rises on stone slabs with weeds in between them, it rises and falls like a battle area. We used to have such good times down here, but now all there is is headaches and self-doubt. Oh well. But this courtyard, it used to be a warzone. I watch it like a little model village, all full of intricacies. But there is nothing here really and it is all just me, ill-judged and ill-thought. This little corner exists and the tree exists, and the world goes on around it, but it is untouched and hardly seen. There is a humming, something around the classroom doors. A sparrow darts across the courtyard, nestles behind the metallic art installation hung up by art students. Another sparrow joins it behind. They are gone for a long time. Perhaps they are making love. Those art students, they are beautiful and enviable people – goddamn. And perhaps it's all adolescent silliness, and on closer thought, what else could it be? But there is no such thing as adult thoughts, and everyone is a clumsy whale. No one knows what's going to happen to anyone and everything is being swept away, always. There is always an opposing view. But maybe I could still date one of those artists, one day. Painters, photographers. Not only would they be pretty but they wouldn't push me in any kind of direction, which is always a danger in relationships. People have these grand expectations. Nevertheless, there's a wall in me, and life is already gruelling enough – photos, stones in shoes. There's so much to remember. The sparrows come out from the artwork, seemingly with crowns on their heads, the dominant and irrepressible spirit of nature. One flies away, over roofs, and goes somewhere else. The other is left on the floor by the bench away from me, and it hops around, curious, and nosing at the ground. I am losing that same curiosity, it is not something that sustains. The sky is blue and the clouds are white and streaked and stretched thin. The concrete hills of this courtyard dip and overhang. I get distracted and look again and the sparrow is gone. I stand to leave. I know that these times alone do very little, but it is good to have time alone, and by my measure, always bad to spend it with others.

Latticework

Dark castle with dark windows on hill on fire.

Barbed wire lookouts,

mesh.

Burned toast in morning at table,

listening to rationing radio.

The sound of glasses shattering,

beer fights at bars,

a plate stashed into the side of neck.

No attainment out this far,

in golden room, with blonde hair men.

Divested of all politics, all culture, conversation.

Oblivionised by volcanic ash,

needing coffee to stay awake,

amphetamine to sleep,

hurting to have soul still energised.

One gypsy boy with his brain still whole,

falling in love with books with big spines.

But me ruining him as soon as I get the chance.

Putting grubby tongue down his lungs.

Hungry for something decommodified and non-robotized,

leaping on it with viciousness,

impassiveness.

Him suitably disturbed

by the whole latticework of my internal organs.

Flowers

Flowers, I buy flowers and put them in a vase. They are flowers from the store, held in bunches held in plastic. Young people put noses into the flowers, kiss the air with lips smelling of petals. Flowers are for me because I cannot stomach responsibility. I cannot have a dog or cat or boyfriend or child. I would never forgive myself if they died. It's sad when a flower dies, but only so sad. And you can give life to flowers when they're drooping and ill, submerge them in water, make them fat and bloated in vase. I am very nervous but hope to move on with things in life more. I am very far behind. One day I will walk through town, down the ribbon streets and to sea carrying only a bucket and all my possessions. I will head onto ship, stowaway, go out to sea and meditate on the nothingness, the abstract. Spy dolphin pods, blue whales. Return home after years and having seen the whole world. Then I will buy and keep fish. Fish in a fish tank, those are the first steps and it is good to make a plan. Or fish in a flower pot filled with water, if worse comes to worst and there is no other way for them to survive. That will be far enough for first steps. I can dream of children and lovers, love letters, drawings on family fridge. But they can stay as dreams for a while.

Hibernation

I'll die first hopefully.

My mangled mind cannot deal with loss.

The field is a circle inside another circle

and we lay down and fuck in it in dreamscapes.

Me, the French Arab,

and you, the frigid Englishman,

sons of men who hammered at sticks and flags

and ended up blacked out in fields.

I remember now, standing beside coffin lid, your hair like yellow silk,

butter,

your lips very pronounced, belonging in a museum,

cut off and out of your face, mouth.

They're developing some kind of hibernation system for the dead,

some illusory and corporate world.

I only want people to be happy while alive,

not digesting in some fragile permanence of the soul.

But how to be happy and be in love with you when it is all so various?

I want to love you in cold distance,

where you are flushed through fabulously like a painting,

where I can observe like taking a shot with a rifle or a shiny blade,

an arrowhead.

In hot intimate detail, you are overbearing, imperfect,

a flannel of boiling water.

They are inventing a spray for the mind

to channel the ideal and the perfected.

They are modifying it so it can be frosted onto cornflakes or the outside of condoms.

For people into real beauty,

they will receive real beauty,

and for those into real and magnificent horror,

they shall receive also.

I am left remembering your own mangled mind

and your ability to reach me through the porthole,

the illusory dimension.

Such pretty small talk always made small

that I would not tolerate from anyone else.

I think you thought I was small,

too conformist and moderated.

That we were products of fatherly interest

and really should have been friends

outside of this era of relentless espionage where we are
all screaming wolves.

That we gripped gleaming torsos and gun chamber ribs

without really knowing how we felt.

But rest assured,

I will meet you in hibernation,

in the prism of my unending slave life,

when government falls

and regulatory capture of the death industry

is tracked to its natural end point.

When I must wear a shopping channel advert

on my thin morgue stomach

and am raped by fast food companies,

must dye my pubic hair

so to compromise with the virtues of the tabloid
fatherless right,

making love to their own culture war.

And must allow my cheekbones to house coffee shops

for drugged oiks with nothing but commonplace things
to say.

In the final and crushing orbits of cold time,

when even the board of directors cannot rearrange

the universe for fiduciary responsibilities,

I will tell you of how I really thought

and what it was I found so mystical between us

in the days of our fathers and as children

and our expansion into desperate and corrosive
realignment.

Printed in Great Britain
by Amazon

39958212R00030